LILY'S® · KITCHEN ·
PROPER FOOD FOR DOGS

TASTY TREATS
FOR HAPPY DOGS

·········· ❖ ··········

HENRIETTA MORRISON

EBURY
PRESS

Contents

INTRODUCTION 7

Healthy Dog 8

About the Author 12

Avoiding Weight Gain 14

Let's Talk About Teeth 16

When to Offer Treats 18

Vegetarian & Vegan Treats 20

Organic or Not? 21

Essential Ingredients 22

Ingredients to Avoid 26

Storing Treats 28

Useful Equipment 30

1. EVERYDAY TREATS & SNACKS ... 33

2. TREATS FOR PUPPIES & OLDER DOGS ... 65

3. SPECIAL-OCCASION TREATS ... 77

4. ULTRA-HEALTHY TREATS ... 95

Pick-Your-Own Cookies Chart ... 112

Herbal Home Pharmacy ... 114

Energy Requirements for an Active Dog ... 119

The Lily's Kitchen Story ... 120

Index ... 123

Acknowledgements ... 126

Introduction

Healthy Dog

We all love to treat our dogs with morsels of delicious treats, whether as a reward for good behaviour, as coaxing to complete a task, as bribery to come back from the other side of the park or when learning a new trick.

Treats are an intrinsic part of the dog-owner's repertoire, going hand in hand with collars, leads, water bowls, beds, poo bags and food. They are definitely part of the tail-wagging kit. This book is about having fun and helping you to feel confident in making your own fresh, nutritious treats for your dog. You'll discover that they are very easy to make and you can whip up a batch in no time at all.

My dog Lily is a rather fussy border terrier, very picky about what appeals to her taste buds. In fact, she has become even pickier as she has grown older, but that's been rather useful in testing the recipes that follow. You can rest assured that she has given them all her paws-up, and there are no treats in this book that have not passed the Lily Taste Test! Lulu, her granddaughter, is rather different in that she will eat pretty much everything.

> **This book is about having fun and helping you to feel confident in making your own fresh, nutritious treats for your dog.**

Both dogs adore it when I'm in the kitchen cooking, and whilst I was creating the treats and snacks for this book, they both often had flecks of flour on their heads as they

would be carefully positioned right below my mixing bowl, waiting for a taste to come their way. I eventually had to restrict these unscheduled snacks because Lulu started to look a little tubby. Any recipes that didn't work out were instead eaten by my chickens.

More and more pet parents understand that a healthy reward is a worthwhile treat, but trying to distinguish between what is healthy and what isn't can be extremely hard. Most treats are far from healthy, being full of artificial additives and unhealthy ingredients, as well as high in calories. Giving your dog something that is laden with fat, smoked in nitrates or full of chemicals is not exactly a treat. Furthermore, many of the additives are considered to be 'manufacturing aids' rather than ingredients, so they do not need to be legally declared on the label. This is what makes it so hard to be certain about what exactly you are buying.

Many of these chemical additives are used in the manufacturing of treats to give the food structure, shape and stability. They often don't need to be legally declared on the label, as many are classed as 'technological additives', which covers preservatives, emulsifiers, stabilizers, thickeners and gelling agents. Also, if they don't have a legal maximum level for pets, they don't need to be declared.

I firmly believe that we pet parents should trust our nose; if something smells good, it is probably ok, but if it has a rancid, heavily smoked or chemical smell, then it's probably full of things that are not good for your beloved dog. With some treats – those perfectly cut pieces of 'real chicken' or the bright white of 'natural rawhide' – you can tell just by looking that they are artificial. Trust your instincts and avoid any suspect treats.

It's good to know the origin of shop-bought treats so that you can see their provenance and make sure you are happy with the contents. Unfortunately, UK packaging has no obligation to state the country of origin, which makes it very difficult to know where the product was made. If a treat is a bright, glowing colour, then it is not natural and is probably full of chemicals.

Do watch out for 'semi-moist' treats, most of which are soaked in very strong preservatives to prevent them becoming mouldy inside the pack.

Regrettably, there are loopholes that allow manufacturers to call treats 'natural' even though they contain ingredients such as phosphoric acid, artificial antioxidants such as BHA and BHT (found in antifreeze) and potassium sorbate, to name just a few.

The safest solution is to make treats in your own kitchen: it's easy and fun, plus you will know exactly what has gone in the recipe too!

Offering dogs a treat is our way of saying 'I love you'. My heart always leaps when I reach for the jar of treats and both dogs come scampering over and immediately sit down with a thud, as they know that's their polite way of receiving a treat.

And nothing is more satisfying than producing your own jar of fresh treats for your dog (and for gifts too). You know exactly what's gone into them and where the ingredients came from, and you can proudly declare that they originated from 'My Kitchen'.

In these pages you will find lots of ideas, ranging from everyday quick treats to those for special occasions, such as birthdays and

Christmas. You might be unfamiliar with some of the ingredients and not have fed them to your dog before, so if you have any concerns, or fear possible allergies, check with your vet first.

This book is all about celebrating the special bond we have with our furry family, and making the most of all the wonderful, fresh ingredients that are available. I hope this book gives you lots of new ideas for treats and many more special moments with your dog.

> " The safest solution is to make treats in your own kitchen: it's easy and fun, plus you will know exactly what has gone in the recipe too! "

About the Author

I adore my dogs, so much so that I decided to bet my house on starting a pet-food company – **Lily's Kitchen** – that would focus on the best natural ingredients for dogs and cats. I believed there was a need for honest, healthy pet food. Lily, my border terrier, had suffered terribly with itchy skin, 'hot spots', fur loss and a severely decreased appetite. I knew I had to do something about this when I discovered her ailments were down to the pet food I was feeding her.

My brother, who is a vet, encouraged me to venture into the murky world of mass-market pet food (I include veterinary diets here too) and try and make a difference.

Avoiding Weight Gain

It's so tempting to give your pet lots of treats, as who can resist the immediate obedience and intent gaze of a dog giving us their full attention for a small reward?

How to avoid piling the pounds on your hound?

I'm sure I get a little endorphin high when I give a treat to Lily and Lulu; it makes me feel good and it's a joy to see the lip-smacking and general enjoyment they display. We all feel very happy and satisfied with the whole rewarding experience.

However, as pet owners, we do carry a slight feeling of guilt or concern because we know that too many treats can result in a tubby tum and, even worse, joint problems, dental issues and a shortened lifespan. If you have a dog that tends to put on weight, you will need to restrict treats, as some can be very calorific. Treats are snacks, and too much snacking does eventually show on a waistline.

Fortunately, this book is packed with healthy treats, and as long as you are not too generous, all will be well in the waistline department. If you do go overboard on treats (I'm thinking of those times, perhaps in a café, when you want your doggy to stay under the table quietly for a couple of hours – in other words, bribery), you need to provide less food at mealtimes so that the daily calorie intake still stays within safe bounds. I've also included some information on calories, fat and protein for each recipe, which I hope will be helpful.

Let's Talk About Teeth

**Making sure your dog's teeth are in great condition
is a big responsibility for us dog owners.**

I will come clean here (!) – I love brushing Lily's teeth. It is our Sunday morning ritual. I get out the brush, paste, scraper and treats, then she lies in my arms whilst I go around as many teeth as I can get to, including those quite far back. She patiently keeps her mouth open until I have finished, knowing there will be a delicious treat waiting for her when the 'ordeal' is over.

As a frustrated dentist, I am a huge advocate of starting to clean a pet's teeth with a toothbrush when they are as young as possible. With a puppy, you begin brushing for just a few seconds, then give a treat, gradually building up to longer sessions. Lulu is second in the dentist's chair on a Sunday, and she jumps onto my lap with her mouth open, ready for the brushing, as she is so used to it now, plus there's always the treat straight afterwards. If your dog won't tolerate a toothbrush, you could try using a knitted finger cleaner, but I don't find them very effective. Perhaps they are more useful in the early days, when puppies are getting used to you fiddling around in their mouth.

Regular toothbrushing together with a healthy diet and our super Woodbrushes, will ensure your dog's teeth are in great condition. I always blush with pride when the vet checks Lily (now aged 16) and declares her teeth beautifully white and free of plaque. That's down to a great diet (of course) and a weekly tooth scrub.

When to Offer Treats

Treats are all about positive reinforcement, so when
your dog does something you are happy with, a little
treat goes a long way to instil good behaviour and
lovely manners.

I could always guarantee that Lily would return at my call, even in
the middle of Hampstead Heath, as she knew I would have a yummy
treat waiting for her when she came back to me. We were very
diligent with her when she was a puppy – every time she went to her
bed we immediately gave her a treat – and the same applied to Lulu.
Now if they think we have a treat to give, they often run to their
beds to receive it. This happens mostly at night when it's time for
the Bedtime Biscuit!

Size of Treats

Maybe it goes without saying, but the size of the treat needs to match the size of the dog, so please bear this in mind when making the recipes in this book. Everything tends to be 'border terrier' size because of my two dogs, but feel free to increase the size of the treats if you have a bigger dog, and to reduce them if you have a toy breed. You can buy moulds in a variety of sizes, so pick the one that best suits your dog. The same rule applies to quantity: give just enough to make the treats meaningful, but not enough to pile on the pounds. Tiny dogs in particular put on weight very easily, and it's terrible to see an overweight chihuahua, so make only half the recipe. That way the treats will be fresher and won't end up hanging around for too long.

Table Scraps

We sometimes don't think twice about feeding our dog the 'leftovers' after a meal. But you do need to make sure you are not feeding scraps that are salty or peppery. Giving a dog some gravy seems like a lovely idea, but do bear in mind that it will have been seasoned for humans and not for dogs, so it's likely to be far too salty for them.

The other thing to avoid is feeding table scraps that are too fatty, for example the skin of a chicken you've cooked for the family. Doing so could cause a bout of pancreatitis if your dog is sensitive to fat.

Vegetarian & Vegan Treats

> If your dog is on a restricted diet, there are lots of vegetarian recipes you can offer it from this book.
>
> In addition, many of the meat recipes can be adapted to vegetarian or vegan requirements.

For a straightforward vegetarian option, simply omit the meat and add in the same weight of grated vegetables, such as carrots, sweet potato and spinach, plus an egg.

For vegan recipes, omit any cheese (some dogs don't tolerate dairy very well anyway) and add nutritional yeast, which has a cheesy flavour. You can also replace the egg in various doughs with water. It will bind the dry ingredients together, but the dough will be shorter and a bit more brittle to handle.

Organic or Not?

Ideally, you would always use organic ingredients when making food for your dog. Unfortunately, the cost of some organic ingredients can sometimes be rather high, so as long as you are happy with the food choices you are making, then the ingredients you choose will be fine – and still much better than something cooked up by a mass-produced pet-food company (apart from ours, of course!)

. KEY FACTS .

About Organic Ingredients

- Animals that are reared organically have a better quality of life, as they are free to roam outdoors, in their natural habitat.

- No pesticides are used on foods or grass that these animals eat.

- Hormones and antibiotics are not allowed except in exceptional circumstances.

- Organic production usually has a much lower yield, as animals and pastures have not been pumped up with steroids, fertilizers and other artificial additives.

- Organic farming is better for the environment in general – fewer pesticides and artificial fertilizers mean more wildlife and a better overall eco-system.

- Organic certification is a guarantee that no genetically modified ingredients have been used and no artificial ingredients have been used that have not been previously approved by the certifier.

Essential Ingredients

 Most of the ingredients used in this book are easy to find at your local shop, while more unusual ones are obtainable online. Those store-cupboard essentials I cook with most frequently are listed below, and I recommend you buy organic if possible.

– APPLE CIDER VINEGAR –

This is thought to be great for overall gut health, itchy skin and to ward off fleas. It does have a strong smell, so can put a fussy dog off its food, but I've generally included it where the smell is a bit more disguised by another ingredient. If your dog doesn't mind it, sneak a teaspoonful into its food once a day, or add to the water bowl. Start with a tiny amount and build up very gradually to a teaspoonful a day. Make sure they are drinking it, and have a bowl of plain water nearby in case they don't like the taste of the vinegar.

– BLACKSTRAP MOLASSES –

I've always been a fan of this ingredient. Apart from having a delicious malty flavour, it contains lots of beneficial minerals, particularly iron, so may be helpful for dogs who are under the weather to regain their strength and vitality. It can also help to make your dog's coat beautifully glossy. It is a sugar, so only use in small amounts.

– CANNABIDIOL (CBD) OIL –

Some dogs benefit from having this oil added to their food, especially if they have joint issues, but do check with your vet first. Lily is a very sensitive dog, so I can't give her more than two drops a day, and sometimes even this small amount is too much for her.

– CINNAMON –

This is a favourite spice of mine. Not only does it smell wonderful and evoke cosy evenings, but it also has lots of healthy properties. It was traditionally used to 'warm the organs' and to help with chronic indigestion, flatulence and even lower back pain. As an anti-inflammatory, it is good for older dogs who have arthritis, and may also help to ward off diabetes. Interesting trials are currently being conducted into cinnamon's potential as a treatment for Alzheimer's and dementia, so it's also worth sprinkling some on your senior dog's supper. Do not confuse with nutmeg, which is very toxic to dogs.

– FLAXSEEDS –

Also known as linseeds, these golden or brown seeds are a rich source of healthy fats, antioxidants and dietary fibre. They need to be ground in a seed or coffee grinder before being used, as the whole seeds will otherwise pass straight through the gut (as they do in humans). Flaxseeds contain the essential fatty acid omega-3, which is thought to be good for heart function, coats the gut lining and thus helps with digestion, is good for your pet's skin and coat, and provides beneficial fibre. Too much, though, will cause stomach upsets and diarrhoea.

– FLOURS –

Use the flour that is best suited to your dog. I use organic plain flour, as self-raising can contain chemical raising agents that I'd prefer to avoid if possible. If your dog has a wheat allergy, you can use buckwheat, chickpea, potato, amaranth or quinoa flour instead. Be aware that some of these alternatives, such as buckwheat, are more absorbent than regular flour, so you might need to add a little more of them than the recipe specifies in order to get a reasonably firm dough. I recommend buying a seed or coffee grinder – they cost about £15 – and you can then grind your own oats to make flour, or reduce seeds to powder/flour in a flash.

– GARLIC –

Garlic is well known as a natural antibiotic, helping to fight bacterial, viral and fungal infections and supporting the immune system, so I'm glad that my dogs enjoy it (in small amounts). Some say it repels fleas and ticks, but I haven't used it for that purpose, as my dogs are tick magnets and need something stronger. Don't go overboard by giving large amounts of garlic or using it over prolonged periods because it can interact with certain medications, and some breeds, such as akitas and shiba inus, can be very sensitive to it. Always check with your vet before adding it to your pet's diet. Once you have the all-clear, finely chop or crush some fresh garlic and add it soon after preparation so that your pet gets maximum benefit from the active ingredient, allicin. Finally, give garlic only to healthy adult dogs, not puppies or to dogs with digestive disorders, as it may be too strong.

– GINGER –

This warming spice, best known for its anti-inflammatory properties, has the potential to help with arthritis, bloating and travel sickness, so can be useful when you are trying to help a dog who gets car sick. Just remember not to give your dog too much to eat before a car journey, especially if it has a tendency to car sickness. You can mix it with food – a small pinch for small dogs, ½ teaspoon for medium-sized dogs and ¾ teaspoon in larger dogs. Start with a small amount and build up to the full dose.

– KELP –

A seaweed packed with vitamins, minerals and amino acids, this is a fantastic naturally balanced supplement rich in essential nutrients, particularly iodine. Iodine is important for maintaining a glossy coat and healthy teeth and nails. Get the best quality you can find and ensure that it's been harvested from a clean sea. Dried kelp can be kept in a shaker, like salt, and simply sprinkled onto your dog's food every so often.

– NUTRITIONAL YEAST –

A great ingredient for dogs that are sensitive to dairy as it has a cheesy flavour. Sold as flakes or in powder form, it contains lots of amino acids and beneficial minerals. Check the label before buying to make sure it contains vitamin B12, because this is not present in all brands.

– OIL –

I use a range of oils in my recipes. Try to pick the best quality you can, ideally going for cold-pressed oils, which have had less processing. All oils contain essential fatty acids (EFAs), which are essential components of your dog's daily diet. They are crucial to every cell in its body and aid in the regulation of nearly every bodily function. They play a key role in helping to regulate the immune system and can act as powerful anti-inflammatories. EFAs are also important for maintaining a healthy skin and coat, for brain and kidney function and a healthy heart.

The most important families of fatty acids are the omega-3s and the omega-6s. Among the oils used in this book are sunflower oil (a good basic oil), coconut oil (excellent for digestion, fresh breath and shiny coat) and olive oil (great for skin, coat and overall health). You could also opt for flaxseed (linseed) oil, a good source of omega-3 fatty acids, which support the immune system and have anti-inflammatory properties.

– PUMPKIN SEEDS –

Like flaxseeds, pumpkin seeds need to be ground before use so that they don't pass straight through the gut. They are good for overall health and can be helpful as a natural dewormer thanks to the cucurbitin they contain. In fact, due to widespread concern over the resistance of worms and other parasites to conventional medications, much research is being done into the use of pumpkin extracts, and it shows promising results. If you'd like to add ground pumpkin seeds as a daily supplement to your dog's diet, I would suggest a teaspoonful a day for medium-sized (10kg) dogs.

– SPIRULINA –

Like kelp, this is a sea-derived superfood, a 'complete protein', which means it contains all the essential amino acids. I try to use it where possible, but this is tricky, as even the tiniest amount turns food a bluey-green colour. Spirulina is an excellent source of essential fatty acids, carotenoids and many other phytonutrients, which enhance immune function, boost energy levels and support the liver. It is very high in protein and contains a massive array of micronutrients and antioxidants, which are amazing for overall health and vitality.

– TURMERIC –

I'm a firm believer in this yellow spice, known for its anti-inflammatory properties, which has made such a difference to Lily in her older years. It is fantastic for joint stiffness and recovery from joint surgery, and is a great antioxidant. Many dogs will accept it in their food as Golden Paste (see page 75). If not, simply pop a turmeric capsule into their meals once a day. I tend to use an organic form from Pukka Herbs.

– YOGHURT –

The recipes in this book call for natural unsweetened yoghurt or Greek yoghurt. Do not use any yoghurts that contain artificial sweeteners, as these are dangerous for dogs.

> **Do not use any yoghurts that contain artificial sweeteners, as these are dangerous for dogs.**

Ingredients to Avoid

The following items should **never** been given to dogs,
as the consequences could be very serious.

– ALCOHOL –

This has a very toxic effect on dogs and
can make them very sick.

– APPLE PIPS –

Contain very toxic cyanide, so are harmful
if eaten in large quantities.

– ARTIFICIAL SWEETENERS –

Found in many foods such as yoghurts,
cereals etc. Extremely toxic to dogs and can
cause death. Don't even think about giving
your dog any leftover yoghurt if it contains
artificial sweeteners.

– AVOCADO –

Contains persin, which is poisonous
to dogs.

– CHOCOLATE –

Contains theobromine, which dogs find
difficult to metabolize, so it can build up
to toxic levels and ultimately cause death.
While carob is safer, why feed your dog
pretend chocolate when there are so many
healthier choices?

– COFFEE –

Caffeine is harmful for dogs and can cause
seizures (avoid things like chocolate-covered
espresso beans, which are particularly toxic
for dogs).

– GRAPES, RAISINS –
& SULTANAS

These can have a mould on them that
makes them toxic to dogs (so remember,
no Christmas cakes, hot cross buns, fruit
cake etc).

— GREEN/UNRIPE TOMATOES —

These contain alpha-tomatine, which in large amounts can cause heart failure. This ingredient is present in small amounts in the fruit, but is particularly concentrated in the stems and leaves. Although ripe tomatoes have minute traces of alpha-tomatine, they are safe to give to dogs.

— MACADAMIA NUTS —

Can cause a toxic reaction, though the ingredient that causes it is not yet known. Sensitivity to it varies from dog to dog.

— ONIONS, LEEKS — & CHIVES

Contain an ingredient that can cause anaemia in dogs.

— SALT —

This is difficult for dogs to digest, so putting gravy on your dog's dinner may not be the best idea.

Grain-free?

All dogs seem to be going grain-free nowadays. If your vet hasn't specified that your dog should be kept gluten- or grain-free, and you don't mind it having the odd bit of good-quality grain, feel free to make my recipes as I've made them. If you prefer to have grain-free recipes, simply replace any oats and grain flours with buckwheat flour or even potato flour. You might need to adjust the liquids slightly, adding a bit more water or oil to get the desired consistency. Just so you know, I've included plenty of recipes that are grain-free so that no such adjustments are required.

Storing Treats

As all the treats in this book are freshly made with fresh ingredients, wait for them to cool (if taken from the oven), then pop them into sealable freezer bags, lidded plastic boxes or clean screwtop jars and store in the fridge or a cool kitchen cupboard for up to two weeks. Note that treats with a high content of meat, fish or egg should always be stored in the fridge (unless dehydrated). If you have any doubts about the freshness of the treats, err on the side of caution and discard them in case your dog gets an upset stomach.

If you have too many treats to use within the storage time, split the batch and put half in the freezer for later use. When needed, allow to defrost in the fridge, then store in the fridge until used up.

Hygiene

Good hygiene is really important when handling fresh raw ingredients. Make sure you wash your utensils and chopping boards thoroughly after use, especially when you've been preparing raw meat and fish.

Useful Equipment

You don't need any special equipment for
making dog treats – you will probably already have a baking
tray. It's fun, though, to have some shaped cutters, which
make the treats a bit special.

> **"You don't need any special equipment for making dog treats."**

The most exciting piece of kit I have in my kitchen is a dehydrator. It's great for drying high-protein foods for Lily and Lulu, but also allows me to dry many things from my vegetable garden, including all my herbs. With meaty treats, it's advisable to put them in the dehydrator at 70°C/160°F for 10–12 hours, then pop them into a conventional oven for 10 minutes at 140°C/115°C fan/275°F/Gas Mark 1 to kill off any potential bacteria.

There are many models of dehydrator on the market, and it's possible to buy one for well under £100. However, if (like me) you are seriously into dehydrating foodstuffs, it's better to invest in something sturdier. They are very convenient to use and foods you want to dehydrate are placed straight onto the trays without the need for greasing.

Of course, it's possible to dry things in a conventional oven, though it does use more energy. Plus you do need to grease or line baking trays with baking paper. Try and space out the treats so that they are not crowded – use a number of trays if you need to. Good airflow is important, so a fan oven is ideal. Set your oven at 70°C/50°C fan/160°F for meats, and lower if you can for fruits. The drying time will vary, depending on your oven type, but it is generally 7–10 hours. Keep an eye on your treats whilst they are cooking in case they show signs of burning or need to be turned over halfway through. The most important thing is to ensure the meaty ones are properly cooked through and show no sign of pinkness when you break them open.

1

Everyday Treats & Snacks

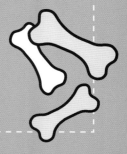

I love having a good choice of treats and snacks for Lily and Lulu – sometimes it feels like it's time for a Doggy Digestive, sometimes a little Liver Treat depending on what we are up to that day. This chapter will give you lots of ideas for treats – the recipes are very simple and you will be delighted with your accomplishments.

More importantly, your dog will be tail-waggingly over the moon to be the recipient of some of your home-cooked snacks. Experiment with the shapes and sizes. Adjust the size of the treat for the size of your dog. If you have a large breed dog, you can double the recipe, as the treats you make will need to be a much bigger size.

Basic Biscuit Recipe

MAKES: 10—12
depending on size

1 tablespoon smooth peanut
butter
1 egg
1 tablespoon water
100g (4oz) plain flour, plus extra
for dusting

ENERGY KCALS/100g: 346
FAT /100g: 10g
PROTEIN /100g: 14g

– VARIATIONS –

• Sprinkle ground flaxseeds
on top.

• Add a grated apple to
the mixture.

This is a great recipe that you can keep as it is or adapt in various ways (see below). To make the biscuits even more appealing, cut the dough into bone shapes if you have a suitable cutter.

Preheat the oven to 180°C/160°C fan/350°F/Gas Mark 4. Grease a baking tray, or line it with baking paper.

Put the peanut butter and egg into a bowl, whisk together with a fork, then stir in the water. Add the flour and mix together to form a dough. Add more water if too dry, or more flour if too wet.

Roll out the dough on a lightly floured work surface until it's about 5mm (¼ inch) thick, then use a cutter to stamp out the shapes you would like. Alternatively, roll the dough into a sausage shape, then cut into slices about the thickness of a pound coin.

Place the shapes on the prepared tray and bake for 30 minutes. Allow to cool, then store in an airtight container in a cool kitchen cupboard. The biscuits will keep for a couple of weeks.

Doggy Digestives

MAKES: 10—12
depending on size

50g (2oz) porridge oats
50g (2oz) oat flour, plus extra
for dusting
50g (2oz) plain flour
1 tablespoon ground pumpkin
seeds
1 tablespoon ground linseeds
100g (4oz) apple purée (see tip)
25g (1oz) coconut oil, melted
1 tablespoon apple cider vinegar

ENERGY KCALS / 100g: 385
FAT / 100g: 18g
PROTEIN / 100g: 9g

– TOP TIP –

To make apple purée at
home: Peel, core and slice a
quantity of apples. Place them
in a large pan and add enough
water to cover. Bring the
water to the boil and gently
simmer the apples for 15
minutes, or until soft. Drain
the apples, then, using a hand
blender, potato masher or
fork, mash into a thick purée.

Sometimes you just need an old-fashioned biscuit that you
know is really healthy for your dog, perhaps because they
are going through a digestive issue or feeling a bit under
the weather. Whatever the case, you will feel proud of
producing a jar of these to sit on your counter, and I bet
you will stop to take off the lid and smell them every time
you walk past!

Preheat the oven to 180°C/160°C fan/350°F/Gas Mark 4.
Grease a baking tray, or line it with baking paper.

Put all the dry ingredients into a bowl. Place the wet
ingredients in a separate bowl, mix thoroughly, then add
to the dry ingredients. As you stir, the mixture should
come together into a very nice firm dough. Add more
water if too dry, or more flour if too wet.

Roll out the dough on a lightly floured work surface
until it's about the thickness of a pound coin, then use
a cutter to stamp out the shapes you prefer. We like to
do a mixture of bones and circles.

Place the shapes on the prepared tray and bake for
about 20 minutes, depending on size. Allow to cool,
then store in an airtight container in a cool kitchen
cupboard. The biscuits will keep for a couple of weeks.

No-Cook Pill Disguisers

. . . . 🐾 . . . .

MAKES: ENOUGH FOR 10 DAYS
depending on size

50g (2oz) smooth peanut butter
1 tablespoon plain flour

. . . .

ENERGY KCALS / 100g: 547
FAT / 100g: 40g
PROTEIN / 100g: 20g

If there's one thing that is a cause of stress in our household, it's how to get Lily to take her tablet. She is incredibly suspicious and on high alert for being tricked by us, so coating the pill in yoghurt or butter or hiding it amongst her food never works. She always seems to spot the disguise, turns her nose up and walks away. Similarly, the vet-bought pill pockets don't work for us, as she doesn't like them.

Fortunately, this recipe seems to be a foolproof way of getting the tablet inside her. It's an absolute life-saver!
If you are treating a dog for pancreatitis, then avoid using this recipe because it is high in fat.

Place the ingredients in a bowl and mix thoroughly until a satisfyingly smooth, mouldable dough forms. Pick off a small piece of the dough and mould it around the tablet that needs to be administered. Give to your dog and feel smug that you have managed to hoodwink it into calmly taking its meds.

This dough can be stored in an airtight container in the fridge for up to 2 weeks.

Homemade Pill Pockets

MAKES: 16
depending on size of dog
and size of pill

225g (8oz) minced lamb or beef
100g (4oz) plain flour
1 tablespoon nutritional yeast
(optional)
5 tablespoons water

ENERGY KCALS / 100g: 245
FAT / 100g: 7g
PROTEIN / 100g: 6g

– TOP TIP –

Minced lamb creates a
lot of fat, so if using lamb,
split the batch between
2 trays.

The recipe opposite works well for dogs that like peanut butter, but if your dog doesn't, you can try this meaty alternative. However, if you are giving medication for pancreatitis, I do not recommend using this recipe because of the fat content – check with your vet if in doubt. If you have to administer pills for only a short period (say, 3–5 days), you can halve the ingredients in this recipe.

Preheat the oven to 180°C/160°C fan/350°F/Gas Mark 3. Grease a baking tray or line it with baking paper.

Place the mince, flour and nutritional yeast (if using) in a bowl and mix together. Add the water and mix again until you have a nice stiff dough. If your mince is quite coarse, you can put all the ingredients straight into a food mixer or processor and mix to create a smoother dough that will be easier to manipulate.

Once you have your dough, break off small pieces (depending on the size of your dog) and roll into balls. Push your finger or thumb partway into each ball to form a pocket large enough to hold the pill. They will end up looking like bonnets, as they will become oval in shape. Arrange them on the prepared tray(s) and bake for 20 minutes.

When you take them out, ensure you can still see the pockets; if not, gently push the handle of a wooden spoon inside to open them up again. This needs to be done while they are still warm.

Allow to cool, then store in an airtight container in the fridge for up to a week. They can be used straight from fridge, or brought up to room temperature, depending on how fussy and suspicious your dog is.

Apple Pie Treats

MAKES: 10—12
depending on size

150g (5oz) buckwheat flour
1 teaspoon ground cinnamon
1 egg
1 teaspoon blackstrap molasses
100g (4oz) apple purée (see
page 36 for homemade)
2 thin slices of apple, cut into
small pieces, to decorate
(optional)

ENERGY KCALS / 100g: 267
FAT / 100g: 4g
PROTEIN / 100g: 10g

These treats smell divine! They somehow have a lovely cosy feeling, and are perfect for making in the autumn, when there are lots of apples that need using up. A wholesome nutritious delicious treat that is a winner with our dogs.

Preheat the oven to 180°C/160°C fan/350°F/Gas Mark 4. Grease a baking tray, or line it with baking paper.

Put the flour and cinnamon into a bowl, make a well in the centre and add the egg, molasses and apple purée. Stir everything together until you have a firm dough.

Break off pieces of the dough (depending on the size of your dog) and roll them into balls. Flatten between your palms, then place them on the prepared baking tray, leaving a thumbprint in the centre of each one. Place a piece of apple (if using) on each print, then bake for about 25 minutes.

Allow to cool, then store in an airtight container for up to a week in a cool kitchen cupboard, or up to 2 weeks in the fridge.

Liver Chip Cookies

MAKES: 12
depending on size

125g (4½oz) oat flour
20g Liver Treats (see page 54),
chopped into small chips
1 tablespoon finely chopped
parsley
1 egg
4 teaspoons water
25ml (1fl oz) olive oil

ENERGY KCALS / 100g: 425
FAT / 100g: 21g
PROTEIN / 100g: 17g

These look just like chocolate chip cookies. The liver I use is dried in a dehydrator, or you can use a conventional oven (see pages 30–1), and I chop them into small 'chips' before adding them to the mixture. The cookies are great for taking out on a walk and firm enough not to crumble in your pocket.

Preheat the oven to 180°C/160°C fan/350°F/Gas Mark 4. Grease a baking tray, or line it with baking paper.

Put all the ingredients into a bowl and mix to form a dough. Roll the dough into a sausage shape about the diameter of a pound coin, then slice into discs about until about 5mm (¼ inch) thick. Place them on the prepared tray and bake for 30 minutes.

Allow to cool, then store in an airtight container in a cool kitchen cupboard for up to 3 days, or in the fridge for up to a week.

Cheese & Apple Puffs

MAKES: 10–12
depending on size

100g (4oz) plain flour
50g (2oz) Cheddar cheese, grated
1 egg
100g (4oz) apple purée (see page 36 for homemade)

ENERGY KCALS/100g: 272
FAT /100g: 10g
PROTEIN /100g: 12g

The combination of cheese and apple has a long history of success at Lily's Kitchen, as it was the basis of the very first treat we sold. This is a slightly different version – a simpler recipe that's a bit more like a cookie. They smell amazing!

Preheat the oven to 220°C/200°C fan/425°F/Gas Mark 7. Grease a baking tray, or line it with baking paper.

Place the flour in a bowl and stir in the cheese. Add the egg and apple purée and mix with a fork until you have a sticky texture that drops off a spoon. Place spoonfuls of the mixture on the prepared baking tray, spacing them about 2cm (¾ inch) apart. Bake for 10 minutes.

Allow to cool on the tray, then store in an airtight container in the fridge for up to a week, or in a cool kitchen cupboard for up to 3 days.

Brownies

400g (14oz) liver (beef, pig's, lamb's or chicken)
2 eggs
200g (7oz) chickpea flour or ordinary flour

ENERGY KCALS / 100g: 226
FAT / 100g: 6g
PROTEIN / 100g: 25g

Although these really do look like chocolate brownies, I'm glad to say they are a much healthier version. It's not the most delightful task to liquidize the liver and eggs, as you get a dark pink liquid that neither looks nor smells terribly appetizing, but that is quickly forgotten when you see how much your dog loves these treats!

Preheat the oven to 180°C/160°C fan/350°F/Gas Mark 4. Grease a brownie tray, small or large, depending on how thick you want the treats to be.

Put the liver and eggs into a blender and whizz for a few seconds to make a thick liquid.

Place the flour in a bowl, add the liver mixture and stir well. Pour into the prepared tray and bake for about 25 minutes. Keep an eye on them, as they need to be cooked but not dry.

Allow to cool, then slice into squares of whatever size you like. Store in an airtight container in the fridge for up to 2 weeks.

Peanut Butter & Banana Bites

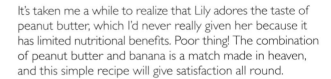

MAKES: 12
depending on size

1 banana
35g (1¼oz) smooth peanut butter
100g (4oz) buckwheat flour or plain flour, plus extra for dusting

ENERGY KCALS/100g: 327
FAT /100g: 9g
PROTEIN /100g: 12g

It's taken me a while to realize that Lily adores the taste of peanut butter, which I'd never really given her because it has limited nutritional benefits. Poor thing! The combination of peanut butter and banana is a match made in heaven, and this simple recipe will give satisfaction all round.

Preheat the oven to 180°C/160°C fan/350°F/Gas Mark 4. Grease a baking tray, or line it with baking paper.

Mash the banana in a bowl, then add in the peanut butter and mix well. Add the flours and mix to form a firm dough. Add a little water if too dry, or more flour if too wet.

Roll out the dough on a lightly floured work surface until it's about 5mm (¼ inch) thick, then use a cutter to stamp out the shapes you would like. Alternatively, roll the dough into a sausage shape about the diameter of a pound coin, then slice into discs, also about the thickness of a pound coin.

Place the shapes on the prepared tray and bake for 25 minutes. If you are making these for older dogs and want them a bit softer, reduce the baking time by a few minutes.

Allow to cool, then store in an airtight container in a cool kitchen cupboard. The bites will keep for up to 10 days.

Fabulous Flapjacks

200g (7oz) porridge oats
50g (2oz) Cheddar cheese, grated
1 heaped tablespoon chopped parsley
100g (4oz) apple purée (see page 36 for homemade)
3 tablespoons sunflower oil
1 egg

ENERGY KCALS / 100g: 321
FAT / 100g: 11g
PROTEIN / 100g: 12g

Here's a fun treat that you can make alongside flapjacks for yourself or your children. Whole, unprocessed oats are great for dogs who have a wheat allergy, as they provide soluble fibre, which is good for the digestion and very nutritious. However, porridge oats are slightly easier to use in this recipe because they have been thinly sliced and form a tighter mixture, making the flapjack a bit easier to cut into squares.

Preheat the oven to 180°C/160°C fan/350°F/Gas Mark 3. Grease a baking tin 20cm (8 inches) square.

Put all ingredients (except the egg) into a saucepan and stir over a low heat for a few minutes until warmed through. Add the egg, stir well, then pour the mixture into the prepared tin. Using a spatula or palette knife, smooth the surface, then bake for 25 minutes.

Allow to cool slightly, then cut into squares of the size you prefer. Set aside to cool completely in the tin. Transfer the flapjacks to an airtight container and store in the fridge for up to 10 days.

Ocean Bars

MAKES: 8
depending on size

30g rolled oats
100g (4oz) plain flour, plus extra
for dusting
1 teaspoon dried kelp
1 x 110g tin tuna, drained
1 tablespoon chopped parsley
5 tablespoons water

ENERGY KCALS/100g: 177
FAT / 100g: 2g
PROTEIN / 100g: 12g

As these are substantial, they're great for taking on a long hike, when you want to reward your dog with a treat that has lots of sustenance, but without a high calorie count. I like to think of it as a doggy version of a sandwich. I take a couple with me for each dog when we are by the sea: I have my egg sandwich and they enjoy their bars, so everyone is happy. Also, I avoid the wide-eyed pleading looks that say 'Please can you share your sandwich with us?'

Preheat the oven to 180°C/160°C fan/350°F/Gas Mark 4. Grease a baking tray, or line it with baking paper.

Put all the ingredients into a bowl and stir until you have a thick but malleable dough. Place it on a lightly floured surface and shape either by hand or with a rolling pin into a long, thin rectangle, depending on the size of the bars you want. I aim for about 1cm (½ inch) thick.

Cut the dough into bars of a suitable size for your dog and place on the prepared tray. Bake for 30 minutes, or 25 minutes if you want a softer texture for a puppy or old dog.

Allow to cool, then store in an airtight container in the fridge for up to a week.

Dried Bananas

MAKES: 1 TRAY

I banana

ENERGY KCALS / 100g: 385
FAT / 100g: 2g
PROTEIN / 100g: 4g

These make great chewy treats, but don't feed your dog too many, as they are high in sugar.

Preheat the dehydrator to 60°C/140°F, or a conventional oven as advised on page 31.

Cut the banana in half, then slice each half lengthways into 3 pieces. Arrange them on the trays, then place in the dehydrator for about 7 hours, or the conventional oven for about 6 hours.

Allow to cool, then store in an airtight container in a cool kitchen cupboard. These treats will keep for 2–3 weeks.

NOTE:

For instructions about using a dehydrator versus a conventional oven, see pages 30–31.

Dried Carrots

MAKES: 1 TRAY

2 carrots, scrubbed clean

ENERGY KCALS / 100g: 186
FAT / 100g: 1g
PROTEIN / 100g: 3g

Preheat a dehydrator to 60°C/140°F, or a conventional oven as advised on page 31.

Cut each carrot lengthways into 4 long sticks. Arrange them on the trays, then place in the dehydrator for about 6 hours, or the conventional oven for 5 hours.

Allow to cool, then store in an airtight container in a cool kitchen cupboard. These treats will keep for 3 weeks.

Dried Apple Rings

MAKES: 4 TRAYS

2 apples

ENERGY KCALS / 100g: 249
FAT / 100g: 2g
PROTEIN / 100g: 0.5g

Preheat a dehydrator to 60°C/140°F, or a conventional oven as advised on page 31.

Core the apples, ensuring no pips are left. You don't need to peel them. Slice into rings about the thickness of a pound coin.

Arrange the slices on the tray(s), then place in the dehydrator for about 9 hours, or the conventional oven for 7 hours – keep an eye on them in case they should start to burn, or need to be turned over, especially if not using a fan oven.

Allow to cool, then store in an airtight container in a cool kitchen cupboard. These treats will keep for 2–3 weeks.

Dried Berries

Follow the instructions above to dry whole raspberries or hulled and halved strawberries. Use them as sprinkles on your dog's food.

SERVING SIZE: ½–1 TEASPOON, AS A TOPPING

ENERGY KCALS / 100g: 221
FAT / 100g: 1g
PROTEIN / 100g: 8g

Beef Jerky

. . . . 🐾 . . . .

MAKES: 12
depending on size

1 teaspoon blackstrap molasses
2 tablespoons apple cider
vinegar
1 x 200g (7oz) piece of chuck
steak, about 5mm (¼ inch) thick

. . . .

ENERGY KCALS/100g: 285
FAT /100g: 8g
PROTEIN /100g: 43g

It's very satisfying to make your own jerky (dried meat),
and it's not as expensive as you might think. Chuck steak
is one of the cheaper cuts, and is nice and lean too, but
you can use whatever cut you like. Just make sure to trim
off the fat. Marinating the meat imparts extra flavour, as
well as extra health benefits.

Put the molasses and vinegar into a shallow non-
reactive bowl and whisk together with a fork until
combined.

Cut the steak into 12 or so slices and place in the
marinade. Cover and place in the fridge for about
an hour.

Preheat a dehydrator to 70°C/160°F, or a conventional
oven to 70°C/50°C fan/160°F.

Transfer the beef slices to the trays, then place in the
dehydrator for 8 hours, or the conventional oven for
about 7 hours (see page 31).

Allow to cool, then store in an airtight container in
fridge. The jerky will keep for up to a week.

Beef Liver Treats

MAKES: ABOUT 40

1 quantity liver (beef, pig's, lamb's or chicken) – I use about 500g (18oz), which makes enough treats for both of my dogs for about 2 weeks

ENERGY KCALS/100g: 500
FAT /100g: 24g
PROTEIN /100g: 70g

Inevitably, a rather strong whiff comes from the kitchen when I make these, but it's very satisfying to fill up a jar with your own meaty treats. The type of liver used is entirely up to you. Beef or ox liver is the cheapest and strongest smelling (which dogs love), and, being large, is very easy to slice into strips and arrange on trays. Pig's liver is also huge, so use that if you find it easier to buy. I generally use chicken livers as I prefer the smell and my dogs like it best.

Preheat the dehydrator to 70°C/160°F, or a conventional oven to 70°C/50°C fan/160°F.

Cut the liver(s) into thin slices (so that they can cook thoroughly) and place them on the trays without crowding. Pop them into the dehydrator for about 10 hours, or the conventional oven for 7–10 hours (see page 31). They should be completely dry, with no pinkness when you cut them in half. When ready, transfer the slices from the dehydrator onto a baking tray and finish them off for 10 minutes in a conventional oven preheated to 180°C/160°C fan/350°F/Gas Mark 3.

Allow to cool, then store in an airtight container in the fridge for up to 2 weeks.

Chicken Jerky

MAKES: 15–20
depending on size

1 skinless chicken breast

ENERGY KCALS/100g: 260
FAT /100g: 2g
PROTEIN /100g: 60g

Most chicken jerky available to buy in the UK does not have a country of origin stamp on the package, so it's impossible to know where it comes from or what additives have been put into the recipe. With this home-made jerky, you'll know exactly where it's made! A simply delicious treat that's ultra healthy and high in protein.

Preheat a dehydrator to 70°C/160°F, or a conventional oven to 70°C/50°C fan/160°F.

Slice the chicken breast along the grain. Each slice should be fairly thin, the thickness of a pound coin. Arrange them on the trays, then place in the dehydrator for about 7 hours, or the conventional oven for 7–8 hours (see page 31). Take a piece out and check that it is completely cooked through by breaking in half and ensuring it is as dry on the inside as on the outside.

Allow to cool, then store in an airtight container in the fridge for up to 10 days.

Banana Muffins

MAKES: 12
depending on size

1 banana
1 egg
1 tablespoon olive oil
1 tablespoon plain yoghurt
100g (4oz) plain flour
1 tablespoon ground
pumpkin seeds
1 tablespoon ground
flaxseeds

FOR THE TOPPING
(OPTIONAL):
2 drops cannabidol (CBD) oil
(optional – see page 22)
2 tablespoons Greek yoghurt,
banana slices or berries
and/or flaxseeds

ENERGY KCALS/100g: 276
FAT /100g: 10g
PROTEIN /100g: 9g

Here's a super-healthy muffin recipe with the benefit of yoghurt. You can also add cannabidol (CBD) oil to the topping, but only if you have the go-ahead from your vet (see page 22). You can spruce up the finished muffins to look more like cupcakes by decorating them with a little dollop of Greek yoghurt and topping them with a small slice of banana or a healthy berry plus a sprinkling of flaxseeds, if you like.

Preheat the oven to 180°C/160°C fan/350°F/Gas Mark 4. Grease a 12-cup muffin tray (or 2 x 6-cup trays).

Put the banana in a bowl and mash well. Add the egg, yoghurt and olive oil and mix together. Add the flour, pumpkin seeds and flaxseeds and mix again until thoroughly combined.

Put a spoonful of the mixture into each muffin cup, then bake for 20 minutes. Allow to cool.

If you want to decorate the muffins, stir the CBD oil (if using) into the yoghurt, then place a dollop on each muffin. Top with a slice of banana or a berry and a sprinkling of flaxseeds.

Tropical Frozen Pops

MAKES: 1 ICE-CUBE TRAY

1 banana
8 raspberries
8 blueberries
6–8 tablespoons water

EQUIPMENT:
Ice-cube tray (12-hole)

ENERGY KCALS / 100g: 49
FAT / 100g: 0.1g
PROTEIN / 100g: 0.4g

– CAUTION –

It's best not to serve ice pops to puppies, as their digestive system can't always cope with very cold items. Instead I'd recommend putting the pop into a bowl of water so that they can still have the fun of slurping but not such a cold hit to their tummy.

I always feel sorry for dogs in warm weather, so I like to give them cold treats throughout the day. When you take the treats out of the freezer, leave them to defrost for about 5 minutes so that they don't end up 'burning' your dog's tongue. Simply put some of the cubes into your dog's bowl and let them slurp or crunch away to their heart's content. If you think your dog is likely to swallow the ice pops whole, crush them up first to make them more like ice shavings. Alternatively, make them in small shallow moulds, or only half-fill your moulds so that the cubes won't present a choking hazard.

These are both very pretty and very healthy. We don't often think about giving our dogs fruit, but it's a great source of vitamin C and antioxidants. Best to feed these when your dogs are out in the garden, as the pink colour can stain.

Mash all the fruit together in a bowl so that you end up with a mixture that's a fantastic pink colour. Add enough of the water to create a loose mixture that's easy to spoon.

Spoon the mixture into the ice-cube tray, filling it only as much as you think safe for your dog. Place in the freezer until set. Serve as described above.

Banana & Yoghurt Pops

These creamy iced treats are great on hot days. Avoid sweetened low-fat yoghurt at all costs, as it may contain artificial sweeteners, which are lethal for dogs.

MAKES: 1 ICE-CUBE TRAY

1 banana
50g (2oz) plain yoghurt
100ml (3½fl oz) water

EQUIPMENT:
Ice-cube tray (16-hole)

ENERGY KCALS/100g: 26
FAT /100g: 0.1g
PROTEIN /100g: 0.1g

Mash the banana in a bowl, then mix in the yoghurt and water until thoroughly combined. Pour into the ice-cube tray, filling it only as much as you think safe for your dog. I recommend shallow filling for smaller dogs in case the cube is too large for your dog to chew. Place in the freezer until set. Serve as described on page 58.

Apple Pops

MAKES: 1 ICE-CUBE TRAY

200ml (7fl oz) apple juice
200ml (7fl oz) water
about 16 small apple pieces
(no pips)

EQUIPMENT:
Ice-cube tray (16-hole)

Combine the apple juice and water in a jug, then pour into the ice-cube tray, filling it only as much as you think will be a safe size for your dog – shallow fill for smaller dogs. Add a piece of apple to each cube, then place in the freezer until set. Serve as described on page 58.

ENERGY KCALS/100g: 26
FAT /100g: 0.1g
PROTEIN /100g: 0.1g

Mince & Mash

· TREATS FOR ·
· COLD DAYS ·

MAKES: 1 SERVING

200g (7oz) potatoes, peeled and chopped
200g (7oz) minced beef or lamb
½ teaspoon ground cinnamon or turmeric (optional)

ENERGY KCALS/100g: 200
FAT /100g: 12g
PROTEIN /100g: 14g

It's lovely to give your dog a warming treat when the weather is really cold. This one is actually more of a meal, but it's not made very often, so it counts as a treat. As many dogs react badly to rice, this recipe is made with potatoes, which are much more soothing if your dog isn't feeling too well. The warmth of cinnamon or turmeric is a nice addition, but the choice is yours.

Cook the potatoes in a saucepan of boiling water for 15 minutes until the point of a knife slips in easily.

Meanwhile, put the mince in a frying pan and cook over a medium heat for about 10 minutes until brown.

Drain the potatoes, keeping a mugful of the water. Tip the potatoes into the mince, add 4–5 tablespoons of the reserved water, then mix until creamy. For an extra feeling of warmth, stir in the cinnamon or turmeric, if you like. Set aside to cool down a bit, and serve slightly warm.

Soup Bowl

MAKES: 1 SERVING

2 carrots, peeled and chopped
2 medium-sized potatoes,
peeled and chopped
handful of spinach, chopped
1 teaspoon nutritional yeast
(optional)

ENERGY KCALS / 100g: 55
FAT / 100g: 0.3g
PROTEIN / 100g: 1.6g

It's always a good idea to get your dog to eat more veg, and this is an ideal way of doing it on a chilly day.

Cook the carrots and potatoes together in a saucepan of boiling water until soft. Add the chopped spinach and simmer for a few minutes until cooked. Drain, keeping a mugful of the water.

Put the vegetables and a few tablespoons of the reserved water into a blender and whizz until smooth. If your dog might not be too keen on a vegetable-only treat, mix in the nutritional yeast for some extra yumminess. Serve slightly warm.

2

Treats for Puppies & Older Dogs

Puppies need lots of treats as rewards to encourage good manners and lovely behaviour. And those treats need to be extremely yummy to distract them from any potential naughty antics.

Puppies have a lot of growing to do, so they need more calories, proteins and fats than adult dogs. Take care, though, not to overdo it on the fat front, because if they grow big too quickly, this can put too much weight on their joints too soon, and of course there are all the other associated risks of getting tubby.

· · · · · · · · ❖ · · · · · · · ·

Older dogs need lots of extra love and attention. They do everything much more slowly, become more finicky about what they eat, often prefer softer chews, but still need treats that are absolutely yummy. Lily, for example, is sometimes ravenous and can't wait to get at her bowl, but at other times she's very happy to skip a meal. Older dogs do need care and patience, and this is our chance to give back to them in many ways. On the diet front, I like to give her a boost with supplements, so I give her turmeric every day for her stiffening joints. Kelp is also wonderful for her fur.

Do bear in mind that older dogs need slightly fewer calories, as they aren't running around using up lots of energy. It's easy to forget that older dogs need to keep their brains active too, so hiding treats in easy-to-find places (under a tea towel or tucked behind a favourite toy) helps them work at getting the treat, which is more stimulating than just handing them one straight from the jar.

Little Bones

FOR PUPPIES

MAKES: 10–12
depending on size

75g (3oz) plain yoghurt
100g (4oz) plain flour, plus extra
for dusting
1 apple, grated (no pips)
1 tablespoon sunflower oil

ENERGY KCALS / 100g: 244
FAT / 100g: 7g
PROTEIN / 100g: 6g

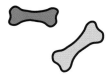

Here's a good treat for an early morning walk. The 'bones' smell absolutely delicious and are very gentle on the stomach. Adjust the size for puppies by cutting the dough into small squares.

Preheat the oven to 180°C/160°C fan/350°F/Gas Mark 4. Grease a baking tray, or line it with baking paper.

Combine all the ingredients in a bowl and mix until you have a lovely soft dough.

Roll out the dough on a lightly floured work surface to a thickness of 5mm (¼ inch) and cut or stamp out bone shapes. Place these on the prepared tray and bake for 25 minutes.

Allow to cool, then store in an airtight container. These treats will keep for a few days in a cool kitchen cupboard, or a couple of weeks in the fridge.

Puppy Power Balls

MAKES: DEPENDS ON PUPPY SIZE

100g (4oz) minced beef
1 apple, grated (no pips)
100g (4oz) plain flour
1 egg

ENERGY KCALS / 100g: 228
FAT / 100g: 6g
PROTEIN / 100g: 13g

It's helpful to have a pile of treats to hand when you are training your pup and need total focus from it. These yummy balls hit the spot. Roll the balls to a size that suits your puppy.

Preheat the oven to 180°C/160°C fan/350°F/Gas Mark 4. Grease a baking tray, or line it with baking paper.

Combine all the ingredients in a bowl and mix until you have a dough.

Break small pieces off the dough and roll them into balls of a suitable size for your dog. Place on the prepared tray and bake for 25 minutes.

Allow to cool, then store in an airtight container in the fridge for up to 5 days.

Puppy Grissini

FOR PUPPIES

MAKES: DEPENDS ON PUPPY SIZE

100g (4oz) minced beef
1 tablespoon nutritional yeast
1 tablespoon ground pumpkin
seeds
100g (4oz) plain flour
1 egg

ENERGY KCALS/100g: 316
FAT /100g: 11g
PROTEIN /100g: 20g

These meaty sticks are a fantastic treat for puppies, as you can keep breaking pieces off while you are training. On the other hand, your puppy will look very cute holding a whole grissini in its paws while gnawing away. I also love it when they run off to enjoy their snack 'privately'. I've included pumpkin seeds here because they can be helpful as a natural dewormer, and puppies do like to scavenge. Grind your pumpkin seeds in a pestle and mortar or grinder to make a crumb-like consistency.

Preheat the oven to 180°C/160°C fan/350°F/Gas Mark 4. Grease a baking tray, or line it with baking paper.

Put all the ingredients into a bowl and mix together to form a firm dough. Break off small amounts of the dough and roll each piece into a cigarette shape (or a cigar if you have a large breed of pup).

Place on the prepared tray and bake for 25 minutes. Don't overcook these unless you want quite a brittle treat.

Allow to cool, then store in an airtight container in the fridge for up to 5 days.

Pup Muffins

200g (7oz) minced turkey
100g (4oz) apple purée (see page 36 for homemade)
1 egg
1 tablespoon sunflower oil
50g (2oz) porridge oats
100g (4oz) plain flour
1 tablespoon ground pumpkin seeds
1 teaspoon dried kelp
small handful of chopped spinach

ENERGY KCALS/100g: 231
FAT /100g: 6g
PROTEIN /100g: 17g

Turkey is a good protein source as it's not too fatty. Together with the spinach and egg in this recipe, it makes a treat with plenty of vitamin E and selenium, both good as antioxidants and immunity boosters. The addition of kelp helps promote a shiny coat and healthy skin.

Preheat the oven to 180°C/160°C fan/350°F/Gas Mark 4. Grease a 12-cup muffin tray.

Place the turkey, apple purée, egg and sunflower oil in a bowl and mix well. Stir in the oats, flour, pumpkin seeds and kelp. Add the spinach and mix thoroughly.

Drop spoonfuls of the mixture onto the prepared tray and bake for 20 minutes.

Allow to cool, then store in an airtight container in the fridge for up to 5 days.

All-In-One Bars

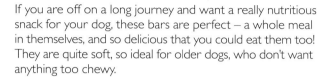

MAKES: 10
depending on size

1 sweet potato, peeled and chopped
2 tablespoons dried red lentils
3 tablespoons porridge oats
2 eggs
1 tablespoon blackstrap molasses
125g (4½oz) minced beef
1 heaped tablespoon plain flour
1 tablespoon chopped parsley
1 tablespoon apple cider vinegar
1 tablespoon olive oil

ENERGY KCALS/100G: 181
FAT /100g: 6g
PROTEIN /100g: 8g

If you are off on a long journey and want a really nutritious snack for your dog, these bars are perfect – a whole meal in themselves, and so delicious that you could eat them too! They are quite soft, so ideal for older dogs, who don't want anything too chewy.

Preheat the oven to 180°C/160°C fan/350°F/Gas Mark 4. Grease a brownie tray.

Put the sweet potato and lentils into a saucepan of water, bring to the boil and simmer for about 15 minutes, until both are tender. Drain, then mash together in a bowl with a potato masher. Stir in the oats and leave to cool slightly.

Whisk the eggs and molasses together in another bowl, then add the mince, flour, parsley, vinegar and oil. Add the potato mixture and stir again. It will be quite wet.

Pour the mixture into the prepared tray and bake for about 50 minutes. If you want a firmer bar, take the tray out of the oven, flip the mixture over, then return to the oven for another 20 minutes.

Allow to cool a little, then cut into squares or rectangles while still warm. Leave in the tray until completely cold, then transfer to an airtight container and store in fridge for up to a week.

FOR OLDER DOGS

Old Dog Muffins

**MAKES: 20 SMALL
OR 12 LARGE**

500g minced turkey thigh meat
1 apple, grated (no pips)
handful of spinach, chopped
2 eggs
100g (4oz) potato, grated
1 teaspoon ground turmeric

ENERGY KCALS / 100g: 529
FAT / 100g: 3g
PROTEIN / 100g: 20g

These muffins have a soft consistency, which is great for older dogs who have lost their teeth or no longer want to do much chewing.

Preheat the oven to 180°C/160°C fan/350°F/Gas Mark 4. Grease 20 cups of a mini muffin tray or trays, or a standard 12-cup muffin tray, whichever you prefer.

Place all the ingredients in a bowl and mix well. Spoon the mixture into the prepared tray(s), being careful not to overfill them or the turkey juice will leak out. Bake the small size for 30 minutes and larger size for 40 minutes.

Allow to cool, then store in an airtight container in the fridge for up to 4 days.

Golden Paste

50g (2oz) coconut oil
1 teaspoon ground turmeric
generous pinch of ground
black pepper

ENERGY KCALS/100g: 875
FAT /100g: 96g
PROTEIN /100g: 0.4g

This bright yellow treat is a must-have for older dogs who have become a bit infirm, stiff or are suffering from arthritis. I have to say it has been a miracle for Lily. She has had three operations on her hind legs, one of which was done incorrectly, so she has ended up with a few screws in her bones. The sad thing is that it's very hard to control a border terrier who is hell bent on chasing squirrels, so she ends up causing herself injuries. Depending on the size of your dog, add ½–1 teaspoon of this paste to their food once a day – and be careful not to get it on your clothes, as turmeric is very hard to wash out.

Combine all the ingredients in a bowl and mix to a stiff paste.

Transfer to an airtight container and store in the fridge for up to 3 weeks.

3

Special-Occasion Treats

It's lovely to include your dog in any special celebrations by giving them their own treats to look forward to. It also means we aren't tempted to feed them human snacks that aren't good for them. You can go to town on these treats and make them as fancy or as simple as you like – either way, your dog will love you even more for them!

Protein Truffle Balls

200g (7oz) minced pork, beef, lamb or turkey
2 tablespoons smooth peanut butter
3 teaspoons nutritional yeast (optional)
2–3 Liver Treats (see page 54, optional)

ENERGY KCALS/100g: 351
FAT /100g: 23g
PROTEIN /100g: 32g

As these really do look like handmade truffles, they make a lovely gift if presented in a glass jar with a ribbon tied around the neck.

Preheat the oven to 180°C/160°C fan/350°F/Gas Mark 4. Grease a baking tray, or line it with baking paper.

Place the meat, peanut butter and nutritional yeast (if using) in a bowl or food processor and mix until a dough forms. Break off small pieces of the dough and roll into balls of a suitable size for your dog.

Grind the dehydrated liver treats to a powder and roll the balls in it. (You can skip this step if you prefer, as your dog will still adore these treats without the coating, but it really does make them look more like chocolate truffles.)

Place the balls on the prepared tray and bake for 25 minutes. Allow to cool, then store in an airtight container in the fridge for up to a week.

Sweet Kisses

150g (5oz) strawberries, large enough to hull
1 tablespoon smooth peanut butter, or cream cheese or plain yoghurt

With peanut butter or cream cheese:
ENERGY KCALS/100g: 250
FAT /100g: 20g
PROTEIN /100g: 9g

With yoghurt:
ENERGY KCALS/100g: 54
FAT /100g: 2g
PROTEIN /100g: 3g

These make a lovely Valentine's treat for your one and only! Or a low-fat summertime treat if you opt for plain yoghurt, which is lower in fat than peanut butter and cream cheese.

Hull the strawberries so that they have a nice deep hole in them.

Using a teaspoon, or perhaps its handle, insert a small amount of your chosen filling into the berries. You can then feed them to your dog straight away – 2 per serving – or freeze them for a summertime treat. If you do the latter, allow them to soften for about 10 minutes before serving to prevent them from being swallowed whole. If you have a dog that is likely to do this, chop the berries into smaller pieces so that they have to be crunched up.

Bonbons

MAKES: 12–18
depending on size

65g (2½oz) smooth peanut
butter
40g (1½oz) coconut oil
½ teaspoon ground cinnamon
or turmeric

ENERGY KCALS / 100g: 800
FAT / 100g: 80g
PROTEIN / 100g: 16g

Dogs adore these sophisticated-looking treats, and they make an ideal gift for dog lovers. Just make sure they stay cool, as they tend to melt easily. (Note that turmeric can stain clothing, so take care when using it.)

Put all the ingredients into a saucepan over a gentle heat, allow to melt, then mix well.

Pour the liquid into sweet moulds that are fairly deep because this makes them easier to turn out without breaking. Alternatively, use a mini muffin tray and pour just a little of the liquid into the bottom of each cup so that you end up with discs. Place in the fridge to set – about an hour.

Store the bonbons in the fridge for up to 2 weeks.

Carrot Cupcakes

MAKES: 12 SMALL OR 8 LARGE

2 carrots, peeled and chopped
2 eggs
2 tablespoons sunflower oil
1 tablespoon ground flaxseeds
1 teaspoon ground cinnamon
100g (4oz) plain flour
blueberries or banana slices,
to decorate

FOR THE ICING:
1 tablespoon Greek yoghurt
1 teaspoon smooth peanut
butter

ENERGY KCALS / 100g: 206
FAT / 100g: 11g
Protein / 100g: 7g

Icing:
ENERGY KCALS / 100g: 230
FAT / 100g: 16g
PROTEIN / 100g: 10g

These are really healthy treats for your dog, and icing them is worth the effort – it not only makes them look great, but adds extra yumminess.

Preheat the oven to 180°C/160°C fan/350°F/Gas Mark 4. Grease a 12-cup mini muffin tray or 8 cups of a standard muffin tray – whichever gives the best-sized treats for your dog.

Cook the carrots in a saucepan of boiling water until tender. Drain and mash, then set aside to cool slightly.

Break the eggs into a bowl, add the oil and whisk together with a fork. Add the flaxseeds, cinnamon and flour and mix well. Add the mashed carrots and mix again.

Place spoonfuls of the batter in the prepared tray and bake for 25 minutes.

Meanwhile, combine the icing ingredients in a bowl and mix until smooth and spreadable.

When the cupcakes are ready, allow to cool in the tray, then turn them out. Spread some of the icing on top of each one and decorate with a blueberry or slice of banana.

Store the cupcakes in an airtight container in the fridge for up to a week, or in a cool kitchen cupboard for up to 3 days.

Surprise Birthday Cake

MAKES: 1 CAKE

1 sweet potato, peeled and
chopped
200g (7oz) minced meat
of your choice
1 tablespoon plain yoghurt
2 eggs
1 tablespoon chopped parsley
1 tablespoon nutritional yeast
(optional)
100g (4oz) plain flour
blueberries or finely chopped
Liver Treats (see page 54),
to decorate

FOR THE ICING:
1 tablespoon Greek yoghurt
1 tablespoon smooth peanut
butter

ENERGY KCALS/100g: 216
FAT /100g: 8g
PROTEIN /100g: 16g

Icing:
ENERGY KCALS/100g: 230
FAT /100g: 16g
PROTEIN /100g: 10g

Compared to humans, our gorgeous dogs are with us for such a short time, so birthdays are occasions to be marked and treasured. However, I remember when my daughter's headmistress, on hearing that we were organizing a picnic for Lily's first birthday, wrote me a letter saying how ridiculous it was to have a birthday party for a dog. I guess it can seem crazy to someone who doesn't have a dog, but we who do regard them as family couldn't imagine not celebrating a family member's birthday.

Preheat the oven to 180°C/160°C fan/350°F/Gas Mark 4. Grease a 450g (1lb) loaf tin and line it with baking paper.

Cook the sweet potato in a saucepan of boiling water until tender. Drain, mash well, then set aside to cool a little.

Put the mince, yoghurt, eggs, parsley and nutritional yeast (if using) into a bowl and mix well. Add the cooled sweet potato and the flour and mix again. Transfer to the prepared loaf tin, level the surface and bake for an hour.

Meanwhile, combine the icing ingredients in a bowl and mix until smooth and spreadable.

When the cake is ready, turn it onto a wire rack to cool. Once it's completely cold, spread the icing on top, then decorate with blueberries or a sprinkling of dried liver.

Slice and serve 1–2 slices at a time depending on the size of your dog. Store any leftovers in an airtight container in the fridge for up to 4 days.

Blender Birthday Cake

MAKES: 1 CAKE

165g (5½oz) liver of
your choice
50g (2oz) apple purée (see page
36 for homemade)
1 egg
2 tablespoons porridge oats
1 teaspoon ground cinnamon
2 tablespoons olive oil
2 tablespoons water
1 large carrot, peeled
1 tablespoon chopped parsley
fresh fruit, to decorate
(optional)

FOR THE ICING:
1 tablespoon Greek yoghurt
1 tablespoon smooth peanut
butter

ENERGY KCALS/100g: 172
FAT /100g: 11g
PROTEIN /100g:: 11g

Icing:
ENERGY KCALS/100g: 230
FAT /100g: 16g
PROTEIN /100g: 10g

This is a super little recipe that's very quick and easy. Handling the liver is rather squelchy, and it can smell pretty strong, especially if using beef or ox liver, but it's worth these slight discomforts because your dog will love it. As the cake is quite rich, don't be tempted to give your dog more than a slice or two at a time.

Preheat the oven to 180°C/160°C fan/350°F/Gas Mark 4. Grease a 450g (1lb) loaf tin and line it with baking paper, making sure it generously overhangs the sides.

Place the liver, apple purée, egg, oats, cinnamon, olive oil and water into a blender and whizz until you have a smooth liquid.

Grate the carrot into a bowl, add the parsley, then pour in the liver liquid and mix well. Transfer to the prepared loaf tin and bake for 45 minutes.

When ready, allow to cool in the tin for a few minutes, then, using the paper overhanging the sides of the tin, carefully lift out the loaf and place on a wire rack until completely cold.

Combine the icing ingredients in a bowl and mix until smooth, then spread on top of the cake. Decorate with fresh fruit, if you like.

Store the cake in an airtight container in the fridge for up to 4 days. Feed 1–2 slices at a time, depending on the size of your dog.

Christmas Dinner Loaf

1 large carrot, peeled
1 sweet potato, peeled
2 Brussels sprouts, finely
chopped
250g (9oz) minced turkey
2 eggs
1 teaspoon ground
cinnamon

ENERGY KCALS / 100g: 118
FAT / 100g: 3g
PROTEIN / 100g: 12g

Here's something that every dog dreams of for Christmas – and it's much healthier than giving them some of your own Christmas feast, which probably contains far too much salt and other flavourings that could cause an upset stomach. Much better to make this loaf for your dog a couple of days beforehand so that you can bring it out and serve them their own slice of Christmas dinner with all the trimmings. Note that this recipe contains no flour, so it really is a meaty loaf.

Preheat the oven to 180°C/160°C fan/350°F/Gas Mark 4. Grease a 450g (1lb) loaf tin and line it with baking paper, making sure it generously overhangs the sides.

Grate the carrot and sweet potato into a bowl. Add the Brussel sprouts and turkey meat and mix well. Add the eggs to the meat mixture along with cinnamon and mix again.

Transfer the mixture to the prepared tin, level the surface and bake for an hour. Pour off any juices that have risen to the surface, then set the loaf aside to cool.

Using the paper overhanging the sides of the tin, lift out the loaf and store it in an airtight container in the fridge for up to 4 days. Feed 1–3 slices at a time, depending on the size of your dog.

Christmas Trees

MAKES: 10–12
depending on size

175–225g (6–8oz) buckwheat
flour, plus extra for dusting
100g (4oz) apple purée (see
page 36 for homemade)
1 egg
1 teaspoon ground cinnamon
dried cranberries, to decorate
(optional)

ENERGY KCALS / 100g: 246
FAT / 100g: 4g
PROTEIN / 100g: 9g

Christmas is foodie heaven in most homes, and while we are spoiling ourselves with lots of delicious festive treats and snacks, it's worth thinking about making some for your dog too so that it doesn't feel left out.

More importantly, it's great to have a jar of doggy treats around so no one is tempted to give your beloved pet things that are meant for humans, such as mince pies, fruit cake, grapes and chocolate, which are all bad for dogs. Also, some human treats (particularly cheese and ham) tend to be high in fat, which could bring on a bout of pancreatitis in your poor dog.

The delicious aroma of these Christmas tree treats will have everyone salivating, and the cinnamon content is full of nutritional benefits for your pet. If you want to make the trees green, add ½ teaspoon of spirulina, but use it carefully, as it can stain clothes.

Preheat the oven to 180°C/160°C fan/350°F/Gas Mark 4. Grease a baking tray, or line it with baking paper.

Put the flour, apple purée, egg and cinnamon into a bowl and mix until you have a firm dough.

Roll out the dough on a lightly floured work surface until it's about 5mm (¼ inch) thick. Using a tree-shaped cutter, stamp out as many trees as you can. If you like, you can decorate the trees with dried cranberry 'baubles'. Place them on the prepared tray and bake for 20 minutes.

When ready, transfer to a wire rack to cool. Store in an airtight container in a cool kitchen cupboard for up to 2 weeks.

Cinnamon Stars

MAKES: 10–12
depending on size

100g (4oz) plain flour, plus extra
for dusting
½ teaspoon ground cinnamon
1 egg
2 tablespoons olive oil

ENERGY KCALS / 100g: 438
FAT / 100g: 21g
PROTEIN / 100g: 12g

Here's another festive winner that your dog or your dog's friends will enjoy.

Preheat the oven to 180°C/160°C fan/350°F/Gas Mark 4. Grease a baking tray, or line it with baking paper.

Combine the flour and cinnamon in a bowl.

Break the egg into another bowl, add the olive oil and whisk together with a fork. Pour into the flour mixture and stir to form a dough. Add some water if too dry, or more flour if too wet.

Roll out the dough on a lightly floured work surface until it's about 5mm (¼ inch) thick. Using a star-shaped cutter, stamp out star shapes. Place on the prepared tray and bake for 20 minutes.

Allow to cool, then store in an airtight container in a cool kitchen cupboard for up to 2 weeks.

(Pictured on page 90)

Festive Turkey Baubles

Quick and easy to make, these turkey treats are ideal for giving to your hound during the festive season, when everyone else is feasting on mince pies and Stilton.

Preheat the oven to 180°C/160°C fan/350°F/Gas Mark 4. Grease a baking tray, or line it with baking paper.

Put the turkey meat, apple purée and cinnamon into a bowl and mix well. (You can use a food processer if you prefer a smoother texture.) Add the flour to form a dough.

Break off small pieces of the dough (suitable for the size of your dog) and roll into balls. Place them on the prepared tray and bake for 25 minutes.

Allow to cool, then store in an airtight container in the fridge for up to 4 days.

MAKES: 8–12

200g (7oz) minced turkey
100g (4oz) apple purée (see page 36 for homemade)
1 teaspoon ground cinnamon
100g (4oz) plain flour

ENERGY KCALS / 100g: 200
FAT / 100g: 2g
PROTEIN / 100g: 18g

4

Ultra-Healthy Treats

Most of the treats and snacks in this book
are very healthy.

I'm passionate about pet owners ensuring they
scrutinize treats labels in the way they do their
dog's main-meal labels. Shop-bought treats often
contain a myriad of unhealthy additives.
By making your own, you know exactly what's
going into them. So if you are looking for ultra-
healthy treats that may also help give some
extra TLC to your dog, then step this way.

Top-of-the-Class Treats

· · · · · · · · · · · · · · ❖ · · · · · · · · · · · · · ·

MAKES: 10
depending on size

10g (¼oz) spinach, finely
chopped
1 carrot, peeled and grated
1 tablespoon finely chopped
parsley
1 tablespoon ground or crushed
pumpkin seeds
1 teaspoon ground turmeric
65g (2½oz) coconut oil, melted
1 egg

· ·

ENERGY KCALS/100G: 332
FAT /100g: 32g
PROTEIN /100g: 5g

There's a powerful punch of turmeric in these treats, which is fantastic for older dogs or dogs with joint issues, and great for humans too! Take care not to feed these on white rugs or pale covers, as any crumbs will leave yellow marks.

Preheat the oven to 180°C/160°C fan/350°F/Gas Mark 4. Grease a baking tray, or line it with baking paper.

Put everything into a bowl and stir until a soft dough forms. Place tablespoons of the mixture on the prepared tray, flattening them slightly as you go to create cookie shapes. Bake for about 30 minutes.

Allow to cool, then store in an airtight container in the fridge for up to a week.

Brighton Rocks

MAKES: 10 –12
depending on size

25g (1oz) porridge oats
2 teaspoons nutritional yeast,
or 20g (¾oz) Cheddar cheese,
grated
100g (4oz) plain flour
2 teaspoons ground flaxseeds
1 teaspoon dried kelp
1 egg
50ml water

ENERGY KCALS/100G: 300
FAT /100g: 6g
PROTEIN /100g: 14g

The kelp in these treats makes them smell like a sea breeze, but it also has many health-giving benefits, as outlined on page 24. Put these tasty bites in your pocket when going on walks, as they don't fall apart and will give your dog something satisfying to chew on.

Preheat the oven to 180°C/160°C fan/350°F/Gas Mark 4. Grease a baking tray, or line it with baking paper.

Combine all the ingredients in a bowl and mix to form a sticky dough. (You might need to add a little more water if not using wheat flour.)

Place tablespoons of the mixture on the prepared tray – they should look like mini rock cakes – and bake for 35 minutes.

Allow to cool, then store in an airtight container in a cool kitchen cupboard for up to 4 days.

Hey Ho M'Hearties!

MAKES: 10 −12
depending on size

100g (4oz) plain flour, plus extra
for dusting
1 tablespoon ground flaxseeds
1 teaspoon dried kelp
2 tablespoons olive oil
2–3 tablespoons water

· ·

ENERGY KCALS / 100G: 440
FAT / 100g: 22g
PROTEIN / 100g: 10g

Here we have some lovely fishy treats with a whiff of kelp, good for windy walks by the seaside. They are quite crunchy, so if you have an older dog who prefers soft treats, bake them for a few minutes less.

Preheat the oven to 180°C/160°C fan/350°F/Gas Mark 4. Grease a baking tray, or line it with baking paper.

Combine the flour, flaxseeds and kelp in a bowl, make a well in the centre and add the olive oil and water. Mix well to form a dough.

Place the dough on a lightly floured work surface and roll into a sausage shape about the diameter of a pound coin. Cut into slices about 5mm (¼ inch) thick. Arrange the slices on the prepared tray and bake for 20 minutes.

Allow to cool, then store in an airtight container in a cool kitchen cupboard for up to a week, or in the fridge for up to 2 weeks.

Blackstrap Biscuits

MAKES: 10
depending on size

100g (4oz) plain flour, plus extra
for dusting
25g (1oz) porridge oats
1 teaspoon blackstrap molasses
1 tablespoon apple cider vinegar
1 egg
2 tablespoons water

ENERGY KCALS / 100G: 288
FAT / 100G: 4g
PROTEIN / 100G: 10g

These are good, healthy treats for all dogs, as blackstrap molasses contains all kinds of vitamins and minerals. They smell delicious too.

Preheat the oven to 180°C/160°C fan/350°F/Gas Mark 4. Grease a baking tray, or line it with baking paper.

Combine the flour and oats in a bowl and make a well in the centre. Add the remaining ingredients to the well, then mix to form a pliable dough. Add more water if too dry, or more flour if too wet.

Place the dough on a lightly floured work surface and roll out until it's about 5mm (¼ inch) thick. Using a cutter, stamp out circles. Place on the prepared tray and bake for about 25 minutes.

Allow to cool, then store in an airtight container. The biscuits will keep for a week in a cool kitchen cupboard, or up to 2 weeks in the fridge.

Fresh Breath Treats

MAKES: 12
depending on size

135g (4¾oz) oat flour
or plain flour, plus extra for
dusting
1½ teaspoons fennel seeds
1 tablespoon finely chopped
parsley
½ teaspoon spirulina (optional,
but recommended!)
4 teaspoons sunflower oil
or olive oil
4 teaspoons water

ENERGY KCALS / 100G: 440
FAT / 100g: 20g
PROTEIN / 100g: 11g

When making these, I wondered whether Lily (very fussy) would turn her nose up, as they contain no yeast or meaty things to entice her. Fortunately, she adores them! The fennel seeds (a useful antioxidant) smell delicious, are good for the digestion and can also help with flatulence and bad breath. The addition of spirulina makes them look very green and very much like treats for teeth.

Preheat the oven to 180°C/160°C fan/350°F/Gas Mark 4. Grease a baking tray, or line it with baking paper.

Combine all the ingredients in a bowl and mix well to form a dough.

Place the dough on a lightly floured work surface and roll into a sausage shape about the diameter of a pound coin. Cut into slices about 5mm (¼ inch) thick and flatten slightly before placing on the prepared tray. Bake for 20 minutes.

Allow to cool, then store in an airtight container in a cool kitchen cupboard for up to a week.

Shiny Fur Balls

MAKES: 12–15
depending on size

small handful of spinach
2 tablespoons chopped parsley
4 tablespoons extra virgin
olive oil
100g (4oz) apple purée (see
page 36 for homemade)
1 tablespoon smooth peanut
butter
1 teaspoon dried kelp
1 tablespoon ground flaxseeds
100g (4oz) oat flour
1 teaspoon nutritional yeast,
plus extra for rolling, if needed
4 drops max cannabidol (CBD)
oil (optional)

ENERGY KCALS/100G: 323
FAT /100g: 21g
PROTEIN /100g: 7g

There is no cooking required to make these treats, which are specially designed to promote healthy skin and shiny fur. The olive oil they contain is also good for intestinal health, but if your dog is prone to pancreatitis, don't give too many, as excessive oil can cause a flare-up. Just one a day is enough for a healthy coat. If your dog is used to cannabidol (CBD) oil, and your vet has recommended it, a few drops can be added to the recipe.

Put the spinach, parsley, olive oil and apple purée into a blender and whizz until smooth. Pour into a bowl and mix in the peanut butter. Add the kelp, flaxseeds, flour, nutritional yeast and cannabidol (CBD) oil (if using). Mix again to form a dough.

Break off small pieces of the dough (suitable for the size of your dog) and roll into balls. If your dog is fussy and can spot a no-meat treat a mile away, roll the balls in some extra nutritional yeast.

Transfer the balls to an airtight container and store in the fridge for up to 2 weeks.

Turmeric Latte

MAKES: 1 SERVING

2 tablespoons plain yoghurt
½ teaspoon ground turmeric
1 tablespoon water

ENERGY KCALS / 100G: 72
FAT / 100g: 3g
PROTEIN / 100g: 5g

– CAUTION –

This is not a human latte.
Please don't serve this hot
to your dog!

I know we don't tend to think about drink treats for dogs, but they're worth a thought, especially this digestive pick-me-up, which contains a shot of turmeric for arthritic dogs. Don't replace your dog's water, though! These drinks should go alongside the regular water bowl.

Combine all the ingredients in a jug, then pour into a dog's bowl and watch your pet lap it up.

Sliced Apples

1 apple, core and
pips removed

ENERGY KCALS / 100G: 53
FAT / 100g: 0.5g
PROTEIN / 100g: 0.6g

If your dog is on a weight-loss diet and you are being really careful not to give high-calorie treats, fresh fruit will be very much appreciated by your dog. You can also offer dehydrated fruit treats (see pages 50–51), which are handy to keep in your pocket when out on walks.

Chop up the apple and place in a plastic bag. You can then use the pieces as training treats or when out on walks. They are also good as a snack.

Fruit Salad

handful of blueberries,
raspberries or strawberries,
hulled, or a mixture

ENERGY KCALS/100G: 31
FAT /100g: 0.3g
PROTEIN /100g: 0.9g

Put or combine the berries in a bowl and give to your dog as a yummy, ultra-healthy snack. Or use berries as training treats or rewards.

Sliced Carrots

1 carrot, peeled

ENERGY KCALS/100G: 35
FAT /100g: 0.4g
PROTEIN /100g: 0.5g

Lots of dogs adore carrots, and like to eat them whole by holding them in their paws and chewing furiously. If you have a dog that is more likely to bite off chunks and potentially choke, slice the carrot lengthways into sticks and feed these instead.

Bone Broth Pops

MAKES: ABOUT 16 CUBES

1 chicken carcass,
or roughly the same amount
of chicken bones

EQUIPMENT:
Ice-cube tray (16-hole)

ENERGY KCALS / 100G: 18
FAT / 100g: 0.8g
PROTEIN / 100g: 2g

– CAUTION –

It's best not to serve ice pops
to puppies, as their digestive
system can't always cope with
very cold items. Instead I'd
recommend putting the pop
into a bowl of water so that
they can still have the fun of
slurping but not such a cold
hit to their tummy.

If you don't have the time or inclination to make your own bone broth, there are some healthy ready-made ones you can buy in the shops. The frozen broth makes a great summertime treat.

Put the carcass or bones into a larage saucepan, cover with water and bring to the boil. Lower the heat and simmer with a lid on for at least 4 hours, but up to 24 hours is ideal (the longer the better so that the collagen leaches out of the bones).

Drain the broth into a bowl, discarding the bones, and set aside to cool. When cold, pour into the ice-cube tray and freeze.

Stuffings for Toys with Holes

It's a good idea to give your dog a chance to work a little bit for rewards. It's much more fun and satisfying than being handed one. Plus they take longer to devour!

Here are some treat ideas for fillings to put into a toy's purpose-made holes. Simply store the toy in the fridge or freezer until required.

1. Plain yoghurt and smooth peanut butter in a 75:25 combination.

2. A tasty scoop of Lily's Kitchen wet food.

3. A low-fat combination of mashed banana and raspberries. This pink mixture is fun, but not if you have pale carpets and covers.

Acid Cider Vinegar Tonic

As with humans, dogs benefit from taking a little cider vinegar every day. It's brilliant for a healthy gut. Start by adding 1 drop to your dog's water bowl every day and gradually build up to a teaspoonful.

PICK-YOUR-OWN *Cookies* · CHART ·

Have fun making your own combination of your dog's favourite ingredients by choosing something from each column.

· FLOUR · (120g/4½ oz)	· OIL · (2 tbsp)	· HERB/SPICE · (½ tsp)	· STAR · INGREDIENT (1 tbsp or as indicated)	· WATER ·
Buckwheat	Coconut (melted)	Cinnamon, ground	Apple, grated (no pips)	2–3 tbsp
Oat	Olive	Kelp, dried	Banana (½), mashed	2–3 tbsp
Wheat, plain	Sunflower	Parsley, chopped	Cheese, Cheddar grated	2–3 tbsp
		Turmeric, ground	Peanut butter, smooth	2–3 tbsp

Combine your chosen ingredients as follows to make about 12 treats.

1. Put the flour in a bowl and make a well in the centre. Add the other ingredients to the well and mix together to form a firm dough. Add more water if too dry, or more flour if too wet.

2. Roll the dough into a sausage shape about 4cm (1½ inches) in diameter, depending on the size you wish, then slice into discs about 5mm (¼ inch) thick.

3. Place on a greased or baking paper-lined baking tray and bake at 180°C/160°C fan/350°F/Gas Mark 4 for 20 minutes.

4. Allow to cool, then store in an airtight container in a cool kitchen cupboard.

Herbal Home Pharmacy

One of the best things about cooking for your dog is that you can tailor the meals to provide what your dog needs at the time and add in some healthy extras, such as herbs and certain spices. (Herbs are the leaves of the plant and spices are from the roots, flowers, seeds, bark or berries of the plant.)

Dogs have evolved to eat herbs in nature over the centuries and indeed I often hear of dogs chewing on rosemary bushes or eating mint from the garden. There's something that feels very naturally nutritious about including herbs in your dog's food.

It's worth remembering that our most commonly used medicines have their origins in the herbs and plants of the natural world.

There are some herbs that I like to use regularly. You're unlikely to grow many of them in your garden, but if you search online you will find several good companies that can supply these herbs to you. Ideally, use organic or wild-crafted herbs that are native to their habitat and have had as little interference as possible and not been exposed to pollutants, pesticides or artificial fertilizers. If you are able to use fresh herbs – for example mint, parsley, rosemary or thyme – so much the better.

As a general guideline, 1 teaspoon of dried is the equivalent of 1 tablespoon of finely chopped fresh herbs. (If you're using ground herbs, you can safely use the same quantity as for dried.)

All the herbs listed here are safe to use at home in moderation. You can buy them in dried or powder form and then mix them together to make your own superfood formulation. Add ½ teaspoon of the mix per day to your dog's home-cooked meal.

– TOP TIP –

Try to use dried herbs that are less than six months old so they still have their potency.

If your dog has a specific medical condition that needs treating, then you should consult a vet who specializes in herbal treatments so that you can be sure your dog is getting the right dosage to help the specific condition that needs treating. If your dog is pregnant, you will need to check whether the herbs you want to use are suitable.

Here is a list of some of my favourite herbs to keep in your store cupboard that are safe to use for most dogs.

You can put a tablespoon of each of the following herbs in a jar and mix them together. Then add in the required amount of your 'superherb' mixture to the recipe.

– ALFALFA –

A bit of a wonder herb, as it contains a good variety of nutrients such as vitamin K, alfalfa can be useful for when your dog is feeling a bit under the weather and is also very high in protein (up to 50 per cent). It is often recommended for stiff joints and dogs with arthritis and to help with mental agility, so is particularly good for older dogs. It is also known as a good treatment for bad breath.

– BURDOCK ROOT –

A herb with lots of medicinal attributes, burdock root is used as a general tonic and can be helpful in treating skin problems thanks to its antifungal properties. It is considered to be a blood cleanser and purifier and a tonic for the liver and kidneys.

– CELERY SEEDS –

Good as a detoxifier, celery seeds are also known to have a calming effect on the digestive system and can be helpful in relieving gas.

– CHAMOMILE –

Chamomile is well known for its calming effects, so helpful in relieving anxiety or to give to dogs that find it difficult to settle at night.

– CHICKWEED –

A soothing herb to help with digestion and stomach upsets, chickweed is also a traditional remedy for arthritis and known for its anti-inflammatory properties.

– CLEAVERS –

Also known as 'Stickyweed', this traditional cleanser is rich in antioxidants including vitamin C, and can help to support the lymphatic system and soothe skin complaints.

– DANDELION –

A very gentle herb with many supportive and restorative benefits, dandelion is packed with many essential vitamins and minerals. Both the leaves and the root can be used as a digestive and liver tonic.

– KELP –
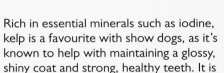

Rich in essential minerals such as iodine, kelp is a favourite with show dogs, as it's known to help with maintaining a glossy, shiny coat and strong, healthy teeth. It is usually easily available as a powder.

– MARIGOLD PETALS –

A good cleansing herb with a brilliant antioxidant action for the organs and skin.

– MILK THISTLE –

A herb that is full of antioxidants and is known for its detoxifying properties, which help to keep the liver healthy.

– MINT –

A beneficial herb for digestion and bloating, mint also helps to freshen breath.

– NETTLES –

A particularly rich source of minerals and vitamins (especially iron), nettles and their phytonutrients can be helpful with skin conditions and allergies. You can also pick your own young nettles – wearing gloves, of course! – cover with water and simmer for 10 minutes. When cool, add a few tablespoons of the liquid and cooked leaves to your dog's food as a good overall tonic.

– PARSLEY –

Parsley is a must-have in your herbal pharmacy: both leaves and stems are very nutritious and contain lots of vitamins, minerals and fibre. Try to use fresh parsley if you can.

– ROSEHIPS –

One of my favourite herbs, rosehips are one of nature's richest natural sources of vitamin C, which helps strengthen the immune system to help keep your dog really healthy. Rosehips are available in ground form from a herbalist, or you can dry your own hips, grind them in a grinder and store in a clean jar in a cool, dark place for up to a month.

– ROSEMARY –

A helpful herb, great for digestion, rosemary is also useful to help calm nerves or an excitable dog.

– THYME –

Thyme can be good if your dog has sore gums, as it has good antiseptic qualities.

– TURMERIC –

This spice is well known for its anti-inflammatory properties and helpful for dogs (and humans!) with arthritis. It is an essential spice for Lily who at 16 has stiffness in her back legs.

Energy Requirements for an Active Dog

It's handy to have a rough idea of how many calories your dog needs every day, although this varies between dogs depending on their metabolism and energy requirements.

You need to take age into account too: old dogs generally need up to 20 per cent less food than younger ones.

The best judge of how much to feed your pet is you. Weighing your dog every month or so will enable you to keep an eye on any weight gain or loss and to decrease or increase the amount you're feeding accordingly. It's also a good idea to get an objective view: we tend to look at our pets adoringly and may not notice if they are a little overweight! Ask your vet's opinion on the weight your dog should be maintaining.

The table here gives an estimate of how many calories your dog should need on a daily basis.

Many of the recipes in the book don't specify definite quantities – this is because treats should be sized according to what is suitable for your dog.

WEIGHT (kg/lb)	ACTIVE Kcal	RESTING Kcal
5 (11)	374	234
6 (13¼)	429	268
7 (15½)	481	301
8 (17½)	532	332
9 (19¾)	581	363
10 (22)	629	393
11 (24¼)	676	422
12 (26½)	722	451
13 (28¾)	766	479
14 (30¾)	810	506
15 (33)	853	533
16 (35¼)	896	560
17 (37½)	937	586
18 (39¾)	978	611
19 (42)	1012	637
20 (44)	1059	662
21 (46¼)	1098	686
22 (48½)	1137	711
23 (50¾)	1176	735
24 (53)	1214	759
25 (55)	1252	782

The Lily's Kitchen Story

My dog Lily was allergic to all the pet foods I bought for her; she came out in rashes and then developed itchy ears and skin. Her fur also never seemed to look healthy. I became obsessed with trying to get to the bottom of why her skin was in such bad condition. My brother, who is a vet, thought it could be related to her food.

So I started cooking for Lily, making her fresh meals every day to see if this would make a difference. Within a couple of weeks, her skin and ears had calmed down, and after another two weeks all her 'hot spots' had disappeared. She stopped looking like a faded old broom and her fur became healthy and shiny. She also lost that rather pungent 'doggy smell', which many owners put up with and eventually become immune to.

Although delighted with the results, however, I was horrified that the food I had been feeding her had been causing these problems. I couldn't believe how blindly I had chosen food for her, believing all the claims on the pack. I felt sure there must be other people like me; indeed, my brother told me that of the numerous pet owners coming into his surgery with their dogs and cats, many had pets with dietary issues.

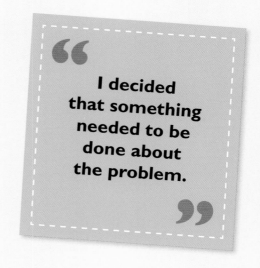

I decided that something needed to be done about the problem.

I decided that something needed to be done about the problem. I wasn't especially keen on cooking for Lily every day; I really wanted something ready-made that I could trust 100 per cent and know would be good for

her. After all, she shows me such devotion and I felt that I had let her down by choosing the wrong food for her.

The next step was spending 18 months talking to a wide range of vets, both conventional and homeopathic, nutritionists and pet-food experts. With their help, I began to put together a list of perfect ingredients for pets, and we started Lily's Kitchen with three recipes. It then took another year to find commercial kitchens who wanted to work with us – most of them turned us down the moment they saw the kinds of ingredients we wanted to make our food with. After visiting more than 30 places, I found the ones that were perfect for us.

We launched in November 2008 and almost immediately had a very loyal following. Like me, many pet owners had struggled to find something really healthy to feed their pets.

People could see this was real food – not 'chunk and jelly' that smelled revolting, or dry food you have to open at arm's length because of the overwhelming smell of rancid grease.

Ten years on, it's wonderful to see the enormous change that has come about in pet food, with lots of natural food choices and pet parents so much more informed and confident about what to feed their pets. I'm proud to say that Lily's Kitchen now employs 60 people – and their 15 dogs! We've won numerous awards and accolades, including, most recently, a Royal Warrant from HRH the Prince of Wales.

We are proud to be a founding member of B Corp in the UK, which enshrines our purpose: business as a force for good, making a difference to our staff, our suppliers, our customers and charities.

This book is based on my experience as a dog owner and my experience in the pet-food industry over the past 10 years. I am not a vet or a qualified nutritionist, so if there are specific dietary questions you have about your dog, please do consult your vet.

FOR MORE ON THE

visit:
lilyskitchen.co.uk

LILY'S KITCHEN RANGE

Index

A

alcohol 26
apple cider vinegar 22
   tonic 111
apple pips 26
apples:
   apple pie treats 41
   apple pops 60
   cheese and apple puffs 43
   dried apple rings 51
   puréeing 36
   sliced 108
artificial sweeteners 26
avocado 26

B

bananas:
   banana and yoghurt pops 60
   banana muffins 57
   dried 50
   peanut butter and banana bites 46
beef, minced:
   all-in-one bars 73
   homemade pill pockets 39
   mince and mash 61
   protein truffle balls 79
   puppy grissini 71
   puppy power balls 68
beef jerky 52
berries, dried 51
birthday cakes:
   blender birthday cake 87

surprise birthday cake 85
biscuits and cookies:
   apple pie treats 41
   basic recipe 35
   blackstrap biscuits 101
   Christmas trees 91
   cinnamon stars 92
   doggy digestives 36
   fresh breath treats 102
   hey ho m'hearties! 100
   little bones 67
   liver chip cookies 42
   pick-your-own chart 112–13
   top-of-the-class treats 97
blackstrap molasses 22
   blackstrap biscuits 101
bonbons 82
Brighton rocks 98
brownies 44

C

cannabidiol (CBD) oil 22
carrots:
   carrot cupcakes 84
   dried 50
   sliced 109
cheese and apple puffs 43
chicken:
   bone broth pops 110
   chicken jerky 55
chocolate 26
Christmas dinner loaf 88

Christmas trees 91
cinnamon 22
  cinnamon stars 92
coffee 26

D
dehydrators 30–1

E
energy requirements 119
equipment 30–1

F
flapjacks 47
flaxseeds 23
flours 23
fruit salad 109

G
garlic 23
ginger 23
golden paste 75
grain-free options 27
grapes, raisins and sultanas 26

H
herbal home pharmacy 114–17
hygiene 28

I
ice pops:
  apple pops 60
  banana and yoghurt pops 60
  bone broth pops 110
  tropical frozen pops 58
ingredients:
  to avoid 26–7
  essential 22–5
  organic 21

K
kelp 24, 112, 116

L
lamb, minced:
  homemade pill pockets 39
  mince and mash 61
  protein truffle balls 79
liver:
  blender birthday cake 87
  brownies 44
  liver chip cookies 42
  liver treats 54

M
macadamia nuts 27
meat, minced:
  surprise birthday cake 85
  see also specific meats
muffins:
  banana muffins 57
  old dog muffins 74
  pup muffins 72

N
nutritional yeast 24

O
oil 24
older dogs 66
  all-in-one bars 73
  golden paste 75
  old dog muffins 74
onions, leeks and chives 27
organic ingredients 21

P
peanut butter and banana bites 46
pill disguisers:
    homemade pill pockets 39
    no-cook 38
pork, minced: protein truffle balls 79
pumpkin seeds 25
puppies 66
    little bones 67
    pup muffins 72
    puppy grissini 71
    puppy power balls 68

S
salt 27
shiny fur balls 105
soup bowl 63
spirulina 25
strawberries: sweet kisses 80
stuffing for toys with holes 111

T
table scraps 19
teeth 16
tomatoes, green/unripe 27
treats 8–11
    shop-bought 9–10
    size 19
    storing 28
    vegetarian/vegan 20
    when to offer 18

tuna: ocean bars 49
turkey, minced:
    Christmas dinner loaf 88
    festive turkey baubles 93
    old dog muffins 74
    protein truffle balls 79
    pup muffins 72
turmeric 25, 117
    golden paste 75
    turmeric latte 106

V
vegetarian/vegan options 20

W
weight gain, avoiding 14–15

Y
yoghurt 25
    banana and yoghurt pops 60

Acknowledgements

I'd like to acknowledge all those at Lily's Kitchen who have enthusiastically supported my vision to create the healthiest pet food on Earth, and have lots of fun on the way. It's easy to have a light-bulb moment, but it's the team around you that makes it possible and provides the magic. I'd particularly like to thank Sophie Giddings and Dan Kimmins for their endless care, brilliance and enthusiasm – they are a dream to work with and I am very lucky to have them on my side.

Thanks also go to:
Holly Mash, holistic vet and homeopath, for her input on all matters holistic. She has been such a help to us over the years with her advice on herbal remedies for pets.

Jeanette Quainton, who is our nutrition specialist and has helped put together the calorific values for the treats in this book.

The team at Ebury Press, who have worked hard behind the scenes to produce this beautiful book.

Petra Börner, who created the original illustration for Lily's Kitchen foods.

My family and friends, especially my brother Bob, the vet who always asks me for proof that my natural approach works. It ensures that we always use ingredients that really do make a difference.

My partner Kim for her support throughout the years, for taking care of our dogs and for creating the space for me to write and research this book.

My daughter Holly for always being enthusiastic and for her sunny-side-up personality, even when the house smells very strongly of chicken livers!

Last but not least, thank you to my dogs – Lily and her granddaughter Lulu. They stuck by me throughout the writing of this book, either under the kitchen counter waiting for a tasty morsel to drop to the floor, or lying next to the table where I was busily scribbling. They adored being Number One and Number Two tasters. I am a nicer person because of the joy and happiness they bring to my life.

1 3 5 7 9 10 8 6 4 2

Published in 2019 by Ebury Press, an imprint of
Ebury Publishing,
20 Vauxhall Bridge Road,
London SW1V 2SA

Ebury Press is part of the Penguin Random House
group of companies whose addresses can be found
at global.penguinrandomhouse.com

Design: Louise Evans
Photography: Haarala Hamilton
Food stylist: Katie Marshall
Prop stylist: Faye Wears
Project editor: Laura Marchant

First published by Ebury Press in 2019

www.penguin.co.uk

A CIP catalogue record for this book is available
from the British Library

ISBN 9781529105506

Printed and bound in Italy by L.E.G.O. S.p.A

Penguin Random House is committed to a sustainable
future for our business, our readers and our planet.
This book is made from Forest Stewardship Council®
certified paper.

*Thank you to all the lovely dogs who appear in this
book — they are some of the dogs that we are lucky
enough to hang out with in the office every day!*